HOUGHTON MIFFLIN

MATH
Expressions
Common Core

Dr. Karen C. Fuson

GRADE

K

Volume 1

This material is based upon work supported by the
National Science Foundation
under Grant Numbers
ESI-9816320, REC-9806020, and RED-935373.

Any opinions, findings, and conclusions, or recommendations expressed in this material
are those of the author and do not necessarily reflect the views of the National Science Foundation.

 HOUGHTON MIFFLIN HARCOURT

Printed in the U.S.A.

ISBN: 978-0-547-82428-4

15 16 17 18 19   0304   21 20 19 18 17

4500675347   B C D E F G

Homework

Draw 5 trees	Draw 3 bees.

Draw 4 rocks.	Draw 2 socks.

On the Back Draw 3 people. Then practice writing the numbers 1 and 2.

1   1   1   1   1   1   1

1   1   1   1   1   1   1

2   2   2   2   2   2   2   2

2   2   2   2   2   2   2

       Count From I to I0

Practice

Go left to right. Ring groups of the number. X out groups that are not the number.

3

4

5

2

➡ **On the Back** Draw a group of 5 squares. Then practice writing the number 3.

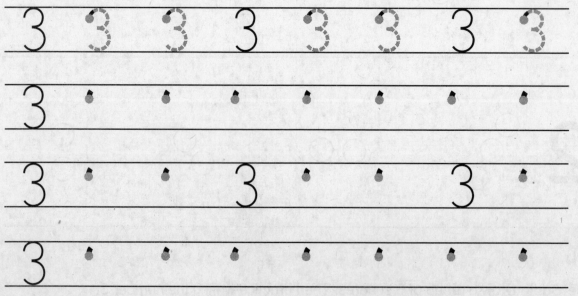

Practice Numbers 1—10

Homework

Name _____

Draw 5 eggs.	Draw 2 legs.
Draw 4 boats.	Draw 3 coats.

➡ **On the Back** Draw 2 goats. Then practice writing the number 4.

Name _____

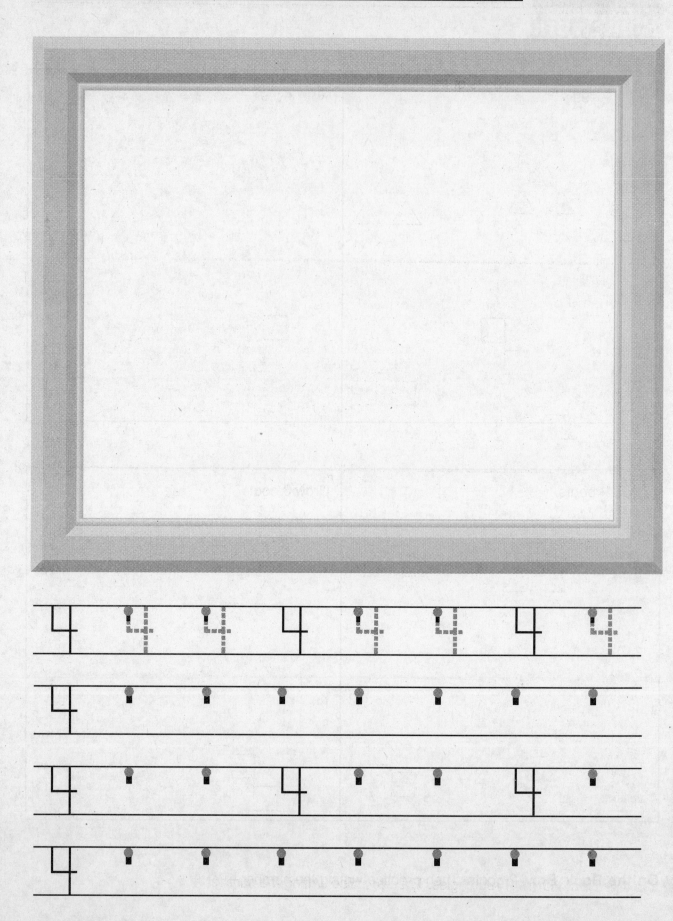

Numbers of Objects in a Group

Go left to right. Circle groups of the number. X out groups that are not the number.

3

4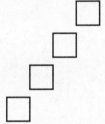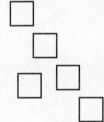

5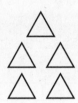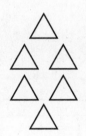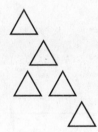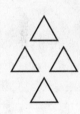

2

➡ **On the Back** Draw 4 rectangles. Then practice writing the number 4.

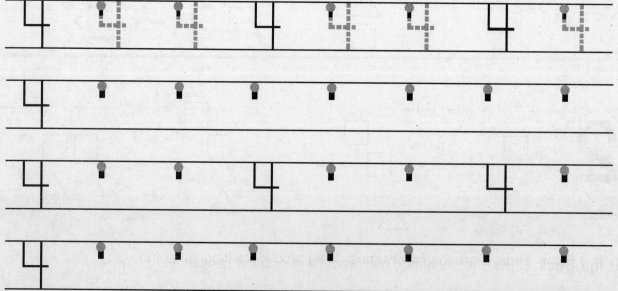

Name _____

Homework

Go left to right. Circle groups of the number. X out groups that are not the number.

3

4

5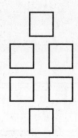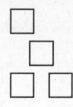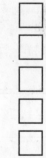

2

On the Back Draw a group of 5 cherries. Then practice writing the number 5.

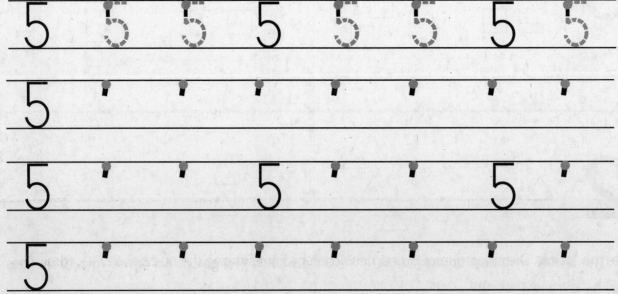

Practice: Number of Objects in a Group

Homework

Connect the dots in order.

● 1   ● 3

● 2

● 2   ● 4

● 1   ● 3

● 2   ● 1

● 3   ● 4

● 1   ● 3   ● 5

● 2   ● 4

On the Back Practice drawing straight lines. Draw lines that go up and down. Also draw lines that go from left to right.

Go left to right. Circle groups of the number. Cross out groups that are not the number.

2

5

4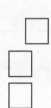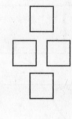

3

On the Back Draw a group of 6. Then practice writing the numbers 1, 2, 3, 4, and 5.

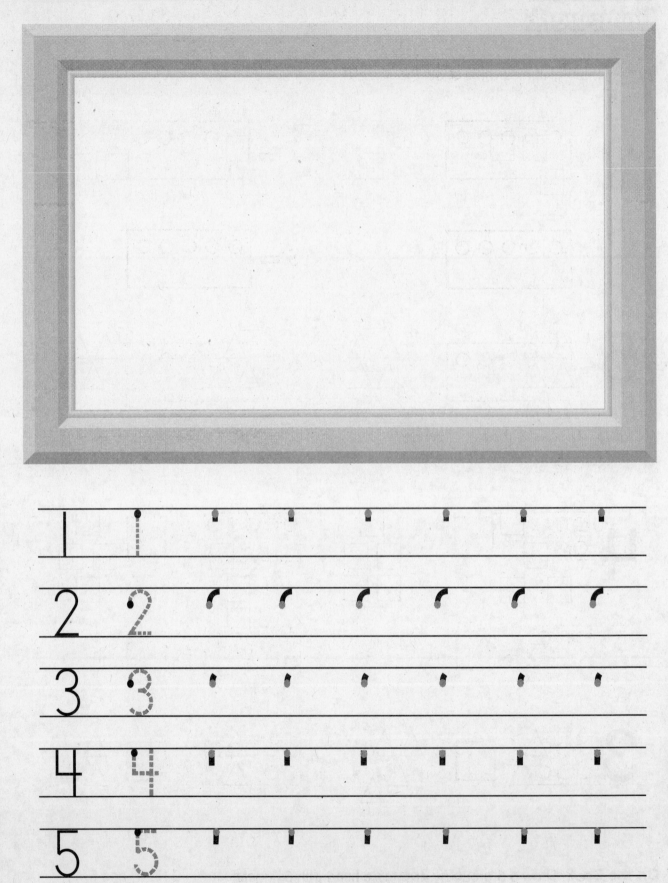

Relate Objects and Numbers 6 –10

Ring groups of the number. Cross out groups that are not the number.

6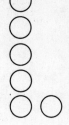

7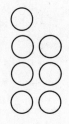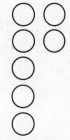

8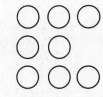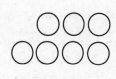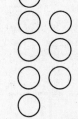

9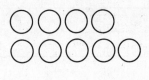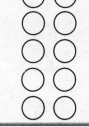

10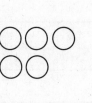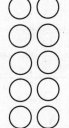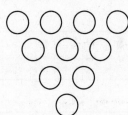

On the Back Draw a group of 6. Then practice writing the numbers 1, 2, 3, 4, and 5.

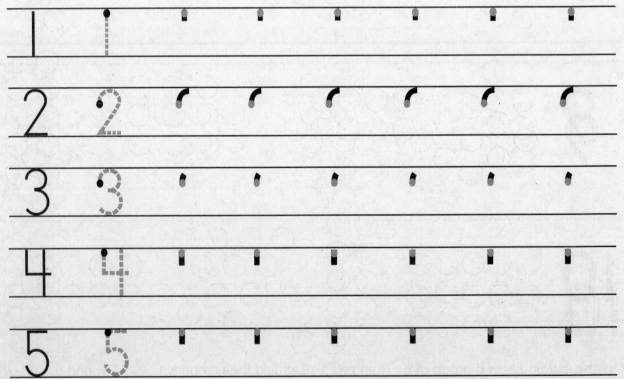

Family Math Stories

Name _____

Ring groups of the number. Cross out groups that are not the number.

6

7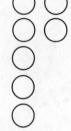

8

9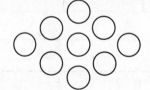

10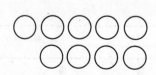

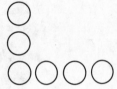

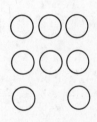

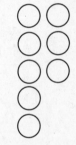

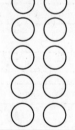

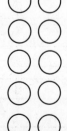

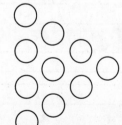

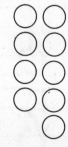

Circle 6 objects from the set below.

Practice writing the number 6.

6 6 6 6 6 6 6 6

6

6 6 6

6

Add and Subtract with Family Math Stories

Homework

Name _____

Practice writing the numbers in order.

| 1 | 2 | | | 5 | | 7 | | | 10 |

| | 2 | 3 | 4 | | | 7 | | 9 | |

| 0 | 1 | 2 | | 4 | | 6 | | 8 | |

| 0 | | | 3 | | 5 | | 7 | | 9 |

Start with 1. Write numbers in order.

| | | | | | | | | | |

Start with 0. Write numbers in order.

| | | | | | | | | | |

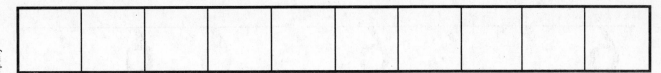 **On the Back** Practice writing the numbers 1–6.

Addition and Subtraction Stories: Playground Scenario **19**

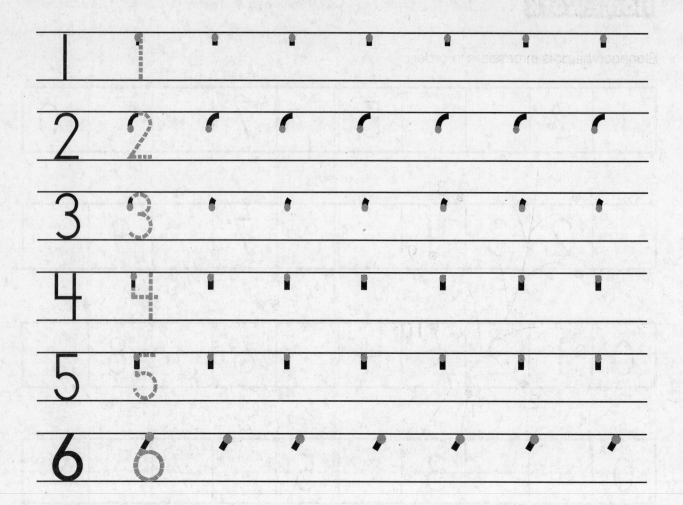

Addition and Subtraction Stories: Playground Scenario

Homework

Connect the dots in order.

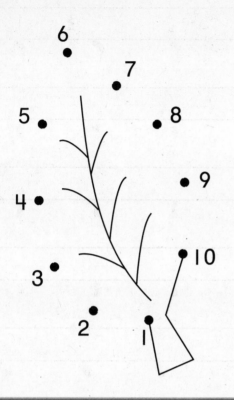

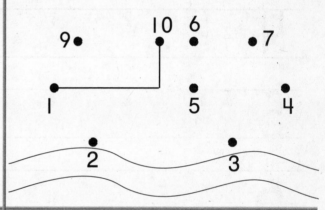

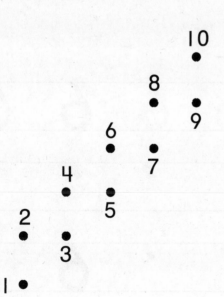

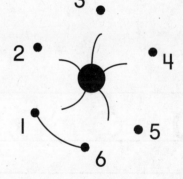

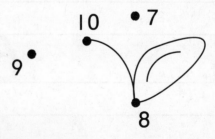

→ **On the Back** Draw 6 flowers. Then practice writing the number 6.

Numbers 6–10

Homework

Name _____

Ring groups of the number. Cross out groups that are not the number.

6

7

8

9

10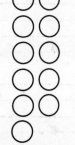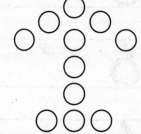

 On the Back Draw a group of 7 rectangles. Then practice writing the number 7.

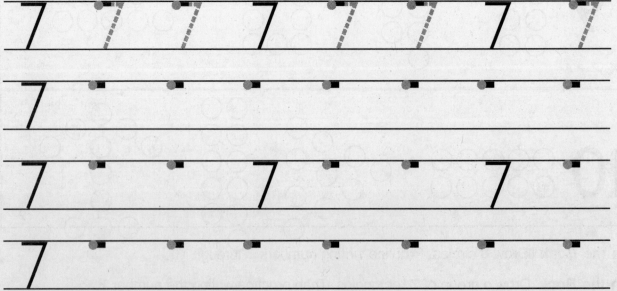

Homework

Draw shapes in each box to show that number.

5	6
7	8

10

⟸ **On the Back** Draw 8 circles. Practice writing numbers 1 through 10.

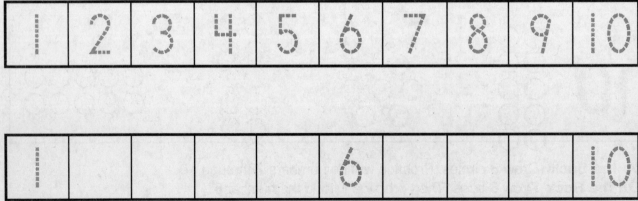

Practice with 5-Groups

Name _____

Homework

Ring groups of the number. Cross out groups that are not the number.

6

7

8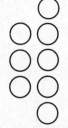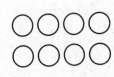

9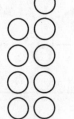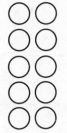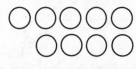

10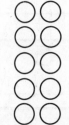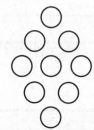

 On the Back Draw 8 bugs. Then practice writing the number 8.

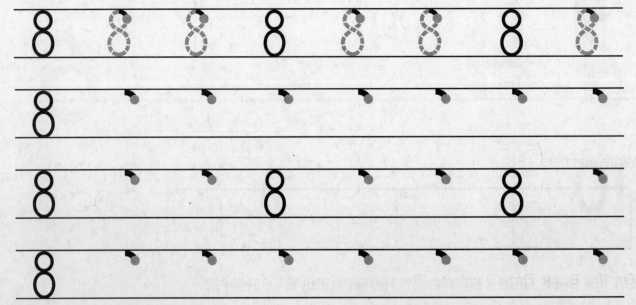

Numbers 6, 7, and 8

Homework

Use a pencil or marker.
Trace each number 2 times.

4	● ● ● ●

6	● ● ● ● ● ●

6 4 6 4 6 4
4 6 4 6 4
6 6 4 4 6 6
4 6 4 6 4 4
6 4 6 4 6
6 4 6 6 4 6

Write numbers 1–8.

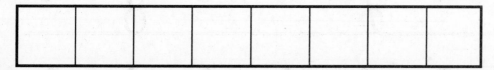

On the Back Draw 9 carrots. Then practice writing the number 9.

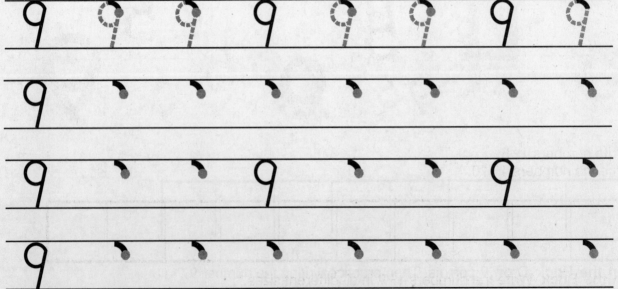

Addition and Subtraction Stories: Garden Scenario

Draw 6 hats.	Draw 9 mats.
Draw 7 cats.	Draw 8 bats.

 On the Back Write the numbers 1–9 in all different sizes.

Numbers 1 Through 10: the +1 Pattern

Homework

Name _____

Circle groups of the number. Cross out groups that are not the number.

6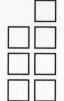

7

8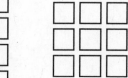

9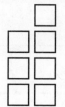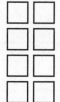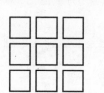

10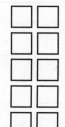

On the Back Draw 9 circles. Then practice writing the number 9.

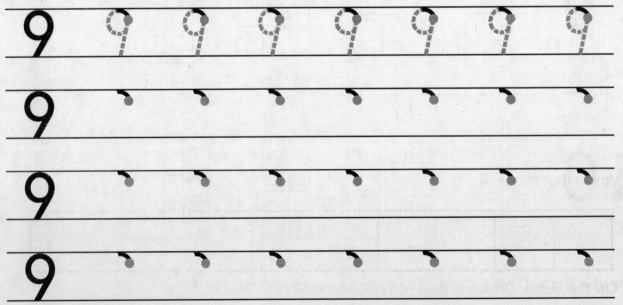

More Numbers 1 Through 10: The +1 Pattern

Homework

Use a pencil or marker.
Trace each number 2 times.

| 4 | ● ● ● ● |

| 8 | ● ● ● ● ●
 ● ● ● |

8
4   8   8
8   4   4   8
8   8   4
8   4   8   4
4   4   8   4
8   4   8
4   8
4   8   4
8   4   8
8   8   4   8

Write numbers 1–10.

➡ **On the Back** Draw a picture of 4 children playing.

© Houghton Mifflin Harcourt Publishing Company

Addition and Subtraction Stories: Family Experiences **35**

Addition and Subtraction Stories: Family Experiences

Homework

Draw 7 cars.	Draw 6 jars.

Draw 9 books.	Draw 8 hooks.

 On the Back Draw a group of 10. Then practice writing the number 10.

Numbers 1 Through 10: The −1 Pattern **37**

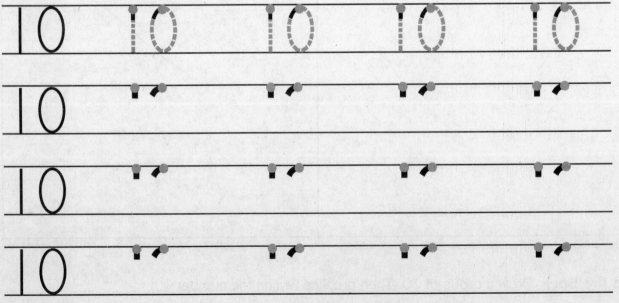

Numbers 1 Through 10: The −1 Pattern

Homework

Name _____

Use a pencil or marker.
Trace each number 2 times.

5	● ● ● ● ●
9	● ● ● ● ● ● ● ● ●

Write the numbers 1–10.

↪ **On the Back** Write the numbers 1–9 in all different sizes.

Number Writing Practice

Homework

Write numbers 4 and 5.

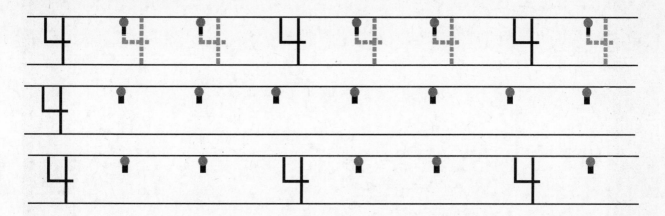

Draw 4 objects.	Draw 4 circles.

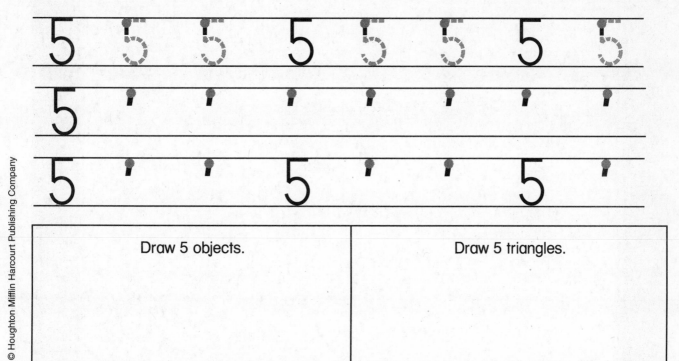

Draw 5 objects.	Draw 5 triangles.

 On the Back Draw 10 animals.

More Numbers 1 Through 10: The −1 Pattern **41**

More Numbers 1 Through 10: The −1 Pattern

Homework

Use a pencil or marker. Trace all the
numbers 2 times.

| 3 | ● ● ● |

| 8 | ● ● ● ● ● / ● ● ● |

8 3 8

3 3 8 3

8 8 3 8 8

3 8 3 3 3

3 8 3 8 3 3 8

8 8 3 8 8

Write the numbers 1–10.

➡ **On the Back** Write the number 8, and draw 8 trees.

Groups of 10 **43**

Homework

Write the number.

1.

2.

3.

4.

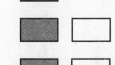

5. Write the numbers 1–10.

 On the Back Draw the pictures.

Draw 7 apples.

Draw 9 squares.

Addition and Subtraction Stories: Park Scene

Write the number.

1.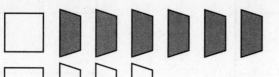

2.

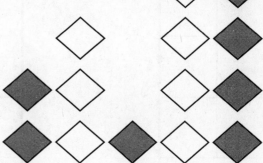

3. Write the number.

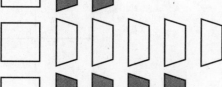

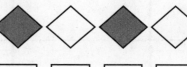

⬭ **On the Back** Write the numbers 1–16.

1	11		1	11			
2	12						
3	13						
4	14						
5	15						
6	16						
7	17			17			17
8	18			18			18
9	19			19			19
10	20		10	20			20

						17	18	19	20

More Addition and Subtraction Stories: Park Scene

Homework

Write the number.

1.

2.

3.

4.

5. Fill in numbers 1–20.

			4	5					
	12					17	18	19	20

➡ **On the Back** Draw 15 crackers.

Homework

1. Write the number. Draw it using the 5-group.

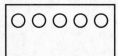

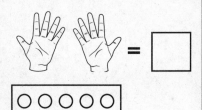

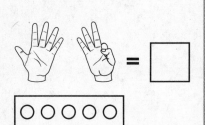

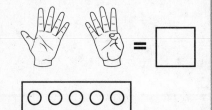

2. Use the 5-group. Draw to show the number.

7 = ⬜〇〇〇〇〇

9 = ⬜〇〇〇〇〇

6 = ⬜〇〇〇〇〇

8 = ⬜〇〇〇〇〇

8 = ⬜〇〇〇〇

10 = ⬜〇〇〇〇〇

10 = ⬜〇〇〇〇〇

6 = ⬜〇〇〇〇〇

3. Write the number.

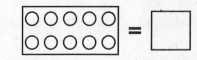 = ⬜   = ⬜

= ⬜   = ⬜

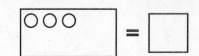 = ⬜   = ⬜

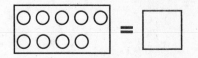 = ⬜   = ⬜

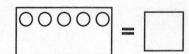 = ⬜   = ⬜

On the Back Draw 16 bananas. Then write the numbers 1 to 16.

						17	18	19	20

Practice Addition and Subtraction Stories: Park Scene

Draw an X over the shape that does not belong.

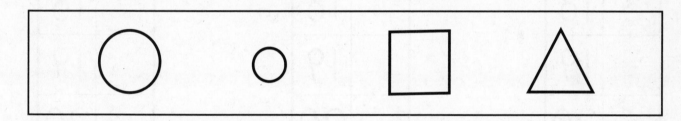

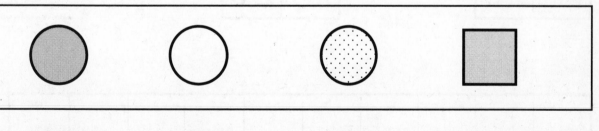

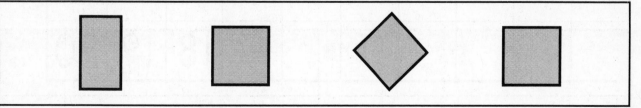

▶ **On the Back** Write the numbers 1–16.

1	11
2	12
3	13
4	14
5	15
6	16
7	17
8	18
9	19
10	20

1	11
	17
	18
	19
10	20

	17
	18
	19
	20

						17	18	19	20

Practice Classifying

Name _____

Homework

1. Use the 5-group. Draw to show the number.

10 = [○ ○ ○ ○ ○]   7 = [○ ○ ○ ○ ○]

8 = [○ ○ ○ ○ ○]   5 = [○ ○ ○ ○ ○]

6 = [○ ○ ○ ○ ○]   9 = [○ ○ ○ ○ ○]

2. Write the number.

[○ ○ ○ ○ ○ / ○ ○ ○ ○] = ☐   [○ ○ ○ ○ ○] = ☐

[○ ○ ○ ○ ○ / ○] = ☐   [○ ○ ○ ○ ○ / ○ ○ ○] = ☐

[○ ○ ○ ○ ○ / ○ ○ ○ ○ ○] = ☐   [○ ○ ○ ○ ○ / ○ ○] = ☐

➤ **On the Back** Show a 5-group by drawing a hand with 5 fingers.
Then write the numbers 1–16.

						17	18	19	20

Build Teen Numbers

Name _____

Homework

1. Draw circles for 1–10.
Show the 5-groups.

1	
2	
3	
4	
5	
6	
7	○ ○ ○ ○ ○ ○ ○
8	
9	
10	

2. Use the 5-group. Draw to show the number.

6 = | ○ ○ ○ ○ ○ |

8 = | ○ ○ ○ ○ ○ |

8 = | ○ ○ ○ ○ ○ |

9 = | ○ ○ ○ ○ ○ |

10 = | ○ ○ ○ ○ ○ |

7 = | ○ ○ ○ ○ ○ |

9 = | ○ ○ ○ ○ ○ |

10 = | ○ ○ ○ ○ ○ |

3. Write the number.

 4. On the Back Draw 7 different rectangles. Then write the numbers 1–16.

						17	18	19	20

Practice with 5-Groups

Homework

Name _____

Write the number.

1.

2.

3.

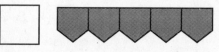 

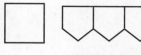 

4. Write the numbers 1–20.

1					7			
		13			17	18	19	20

⬤ **On the Back** Draw 14 socks.

Tens in Teens

Homework

Draw circles to show the partners.

5

5

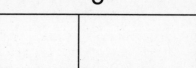

6

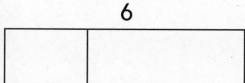

6

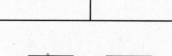

7

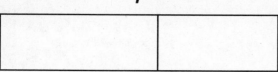

7

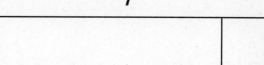

On the Back Write the numbers 1–10 in all different sizes.

　　　　　　　　　　　　　　　　　　　　　　　　　Practice with Partners **61**

1. Draw a circle around a group of 10.

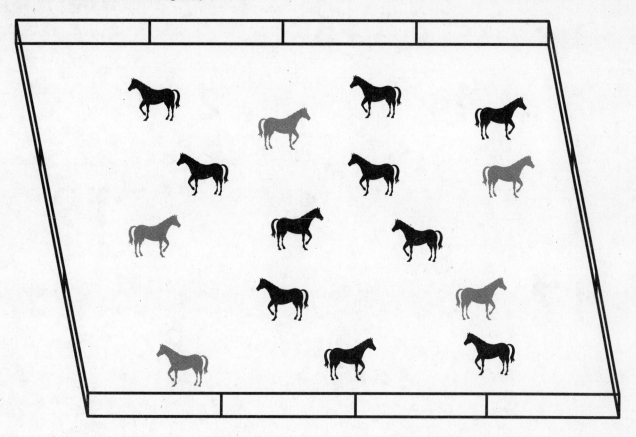

Count how many in all. _____

2. Draw 1 apple for each horse.

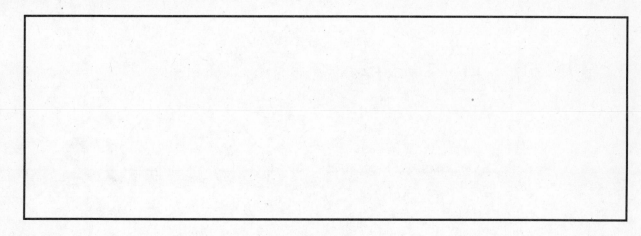

🔵 **On the Back** Draw a circle around every teen number.

13

15

4

1

2

19

9

8

17

6

14

0

5

18

11

16

3

12

7

Show Teen Numbers with Classroom Objects

Homework

1. Write the number. Draw it using the 5-group.

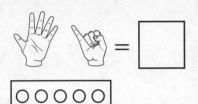

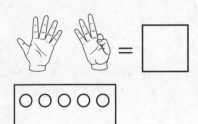

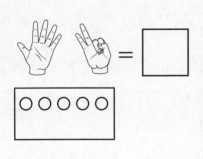

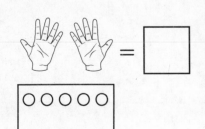

2. Use the 5-group. Draw to show the number.

$10 =$ ⬚ ⬚ ⬚ ⬚ ⬚ (○○○○○) $8 =$ (○○○○○) ⬚ ⬚ ⬚

$6 =$ (○○○○○) ⬚ $6 =$ (○○○○○) ⬚

$7 =$ (○○○○○) ⬚ ⬚ $8 =$ (○○○○○) ⬚ ⬚ ⬚

$9 =$ (○○○○○) ⬚ ⬚ ⬚ ⬚ $7 =$ (○○○○○) ⬚ ⬚

3. Write the number.

[○○○○ / ○○○] = ⬚   [○○] = ⬚

[○○○○ / ○] = ⬚   [○○○○ / ○○] = ⬚

[○○○○ / ○○] = ⬚   [○○○○ / ○] = ⬚

[○○○○ / ○○○○] = ⬚   [○○○○○] = ⬚

🡒 **On the Back** Use shapes to make a picture.

Object Collections: Teen Numbers

Object Collections: Teen Numbers